GERALD GARDNER'S
WHO'S IN CHARGE HERE?
★★★★★★★★★★★★★★★★★★★★★★★★★
CAMPAIGN EDITION
★★★★★★★★★★★★★★★★★★★★★★★★★

BALLANTINE BOOKS • NEW YORK

Library of Congress Catalog Card Number: 80-68314
ISBN 0-345-29463-7

Manufactured in the United States of America
First Edition: August 1980
9 8 7 6 5 4 3 2 1

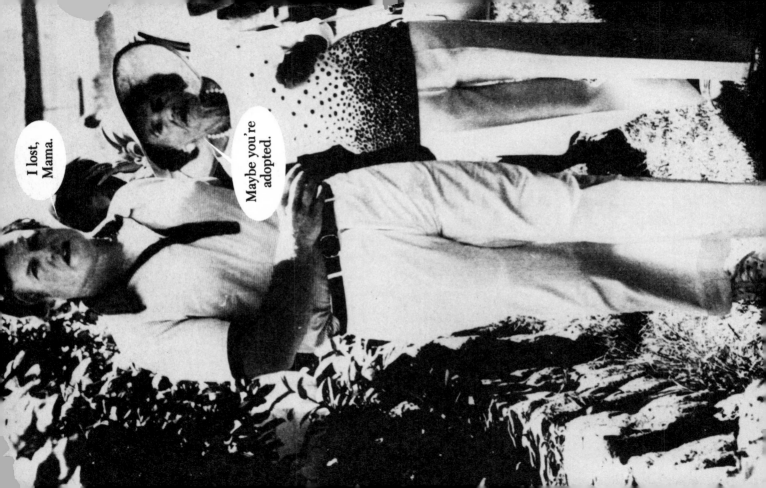

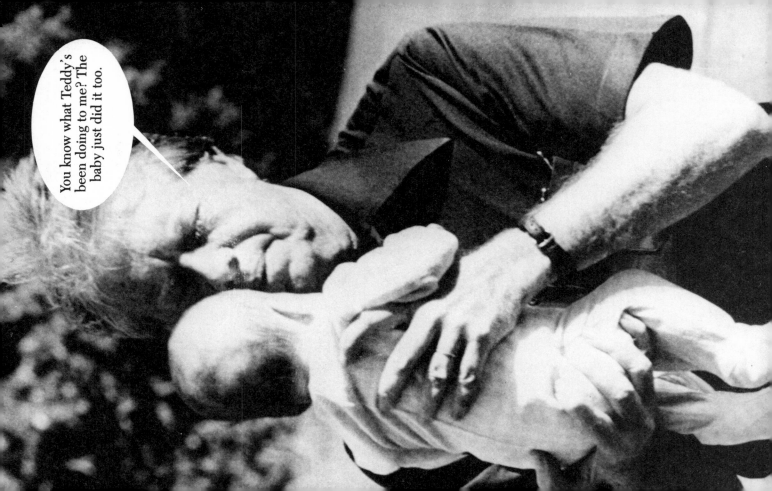

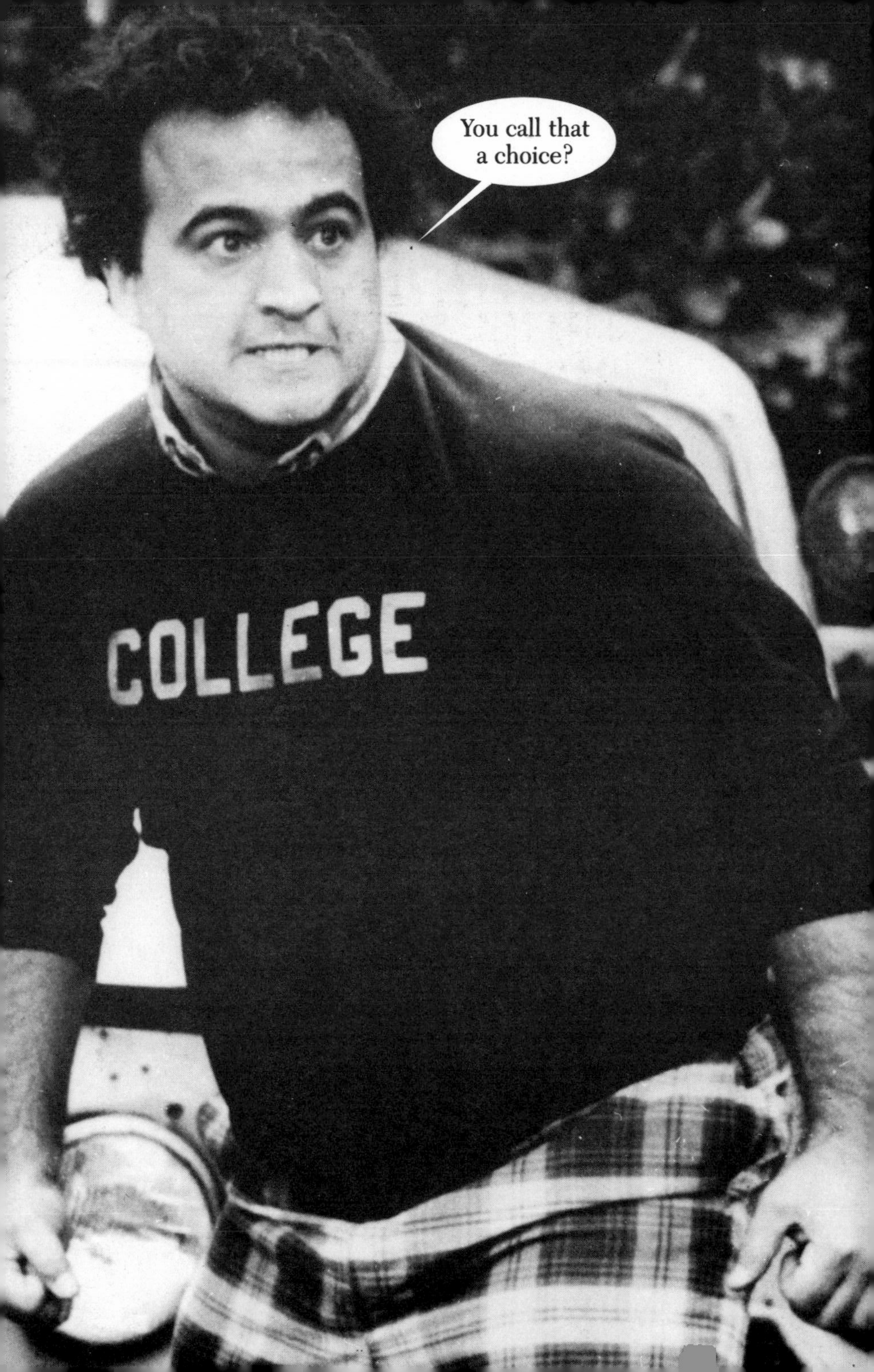
You call that a choice?
COLLEGE

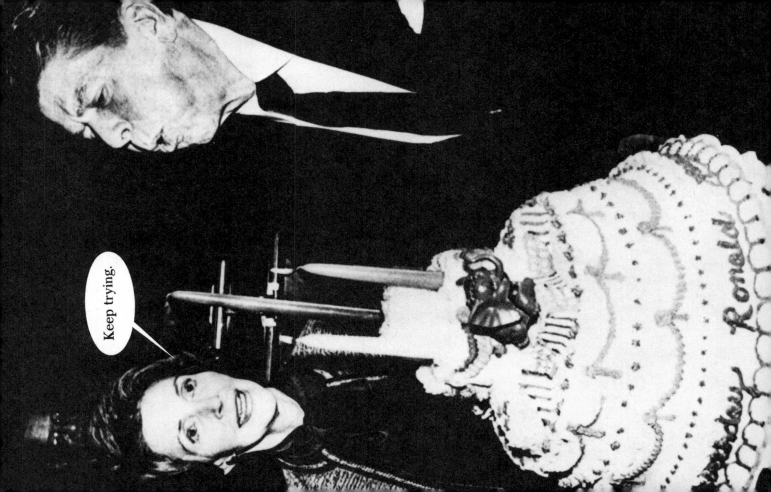

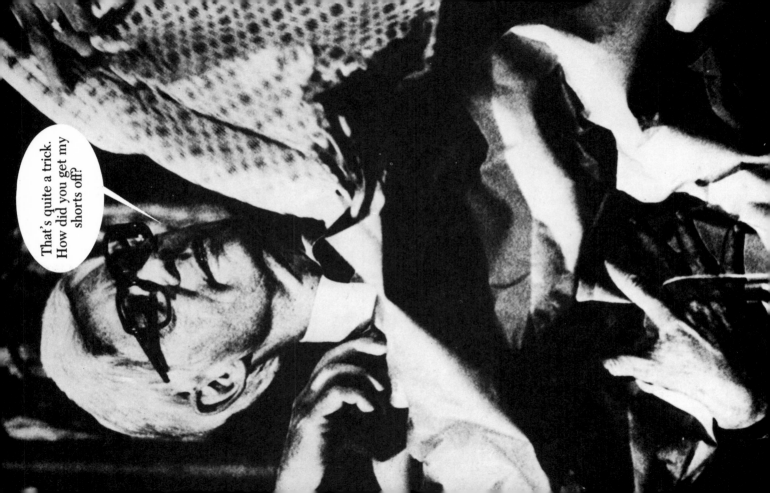

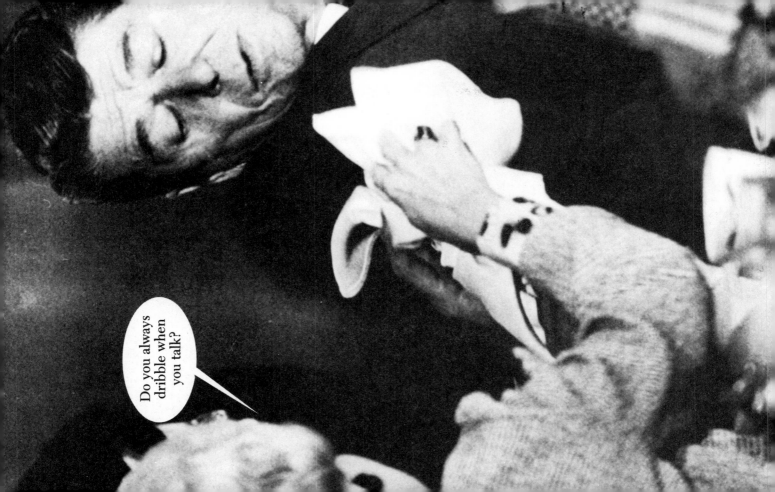

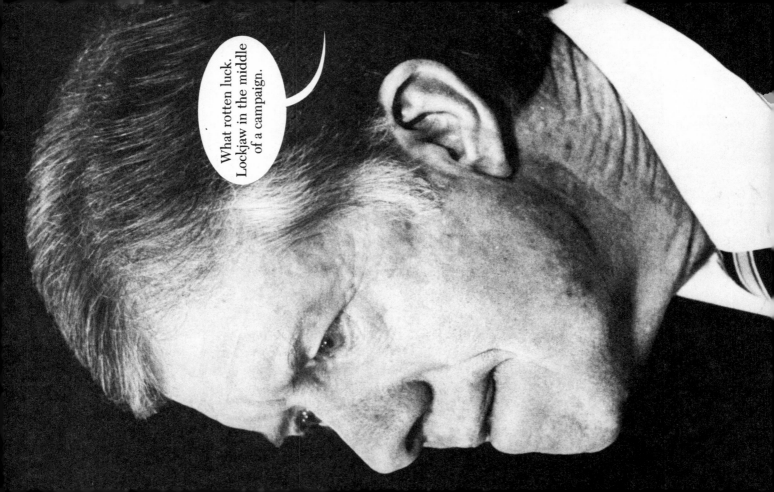

The Royal Family is divided. Philip favors Mr. Carter and I like the other simp.

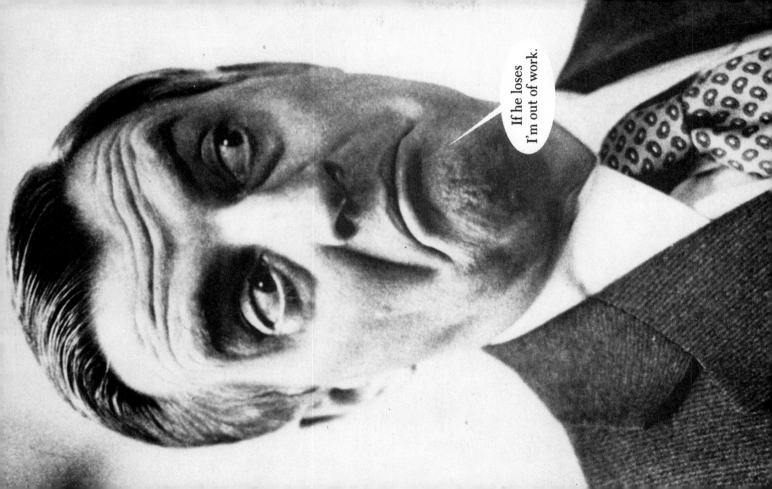

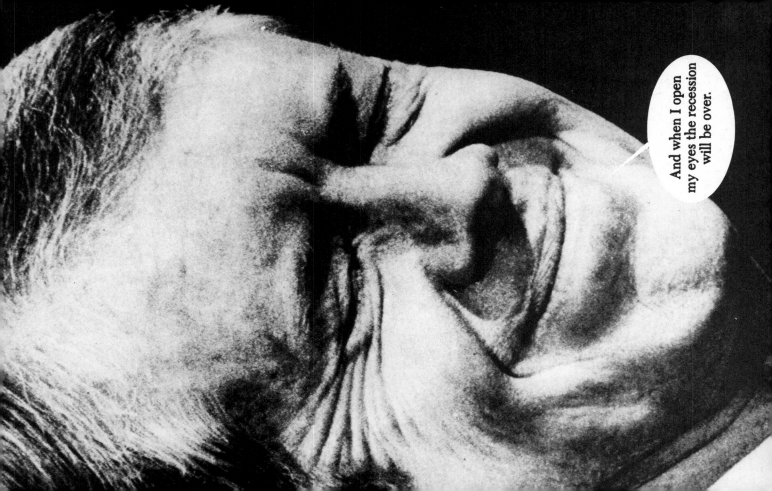

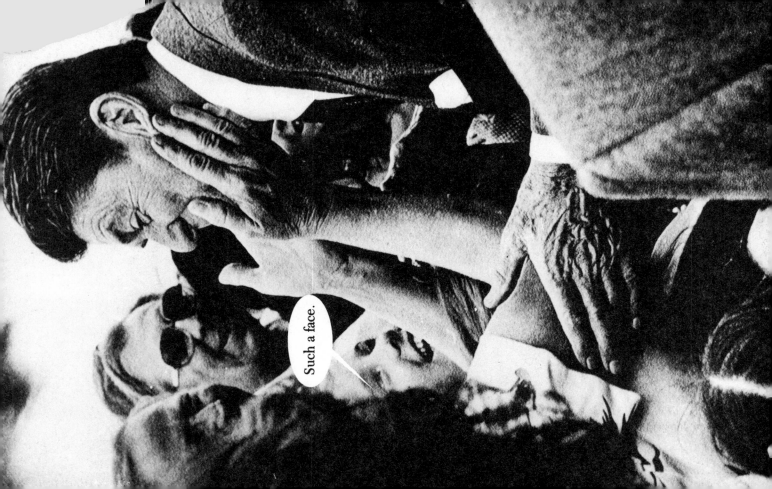

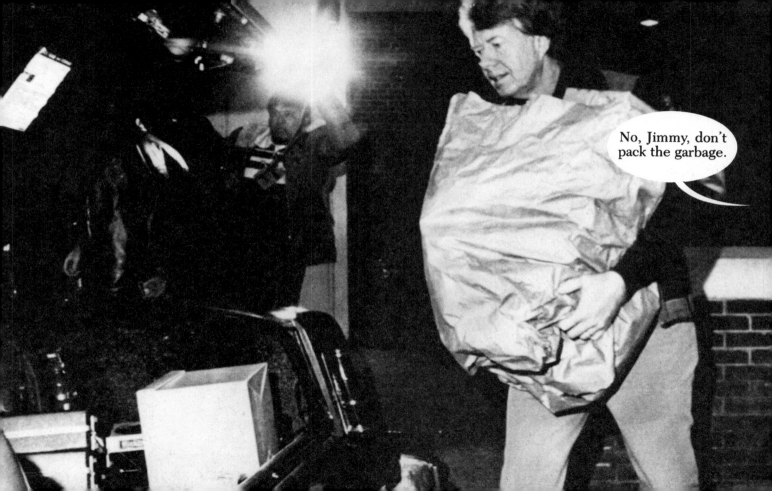

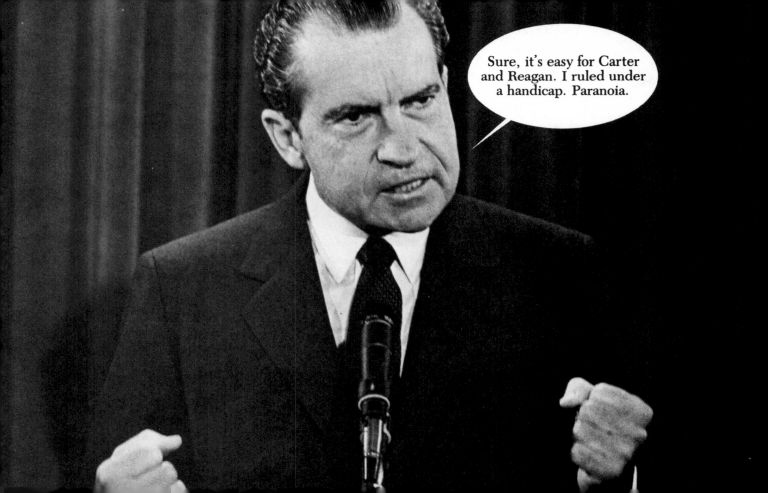